MER   AUG 0 5 20..

35444000516517
j 641.59795 ORR
Orr, Tamra
Pacific Northwest recipes

WITHDRAWN

D0618037

Note: This is a Digital Reproduction Copy of the Original

800-466 VICTORIA STREET
KAMLOOPS, B.C. V2C 2A9

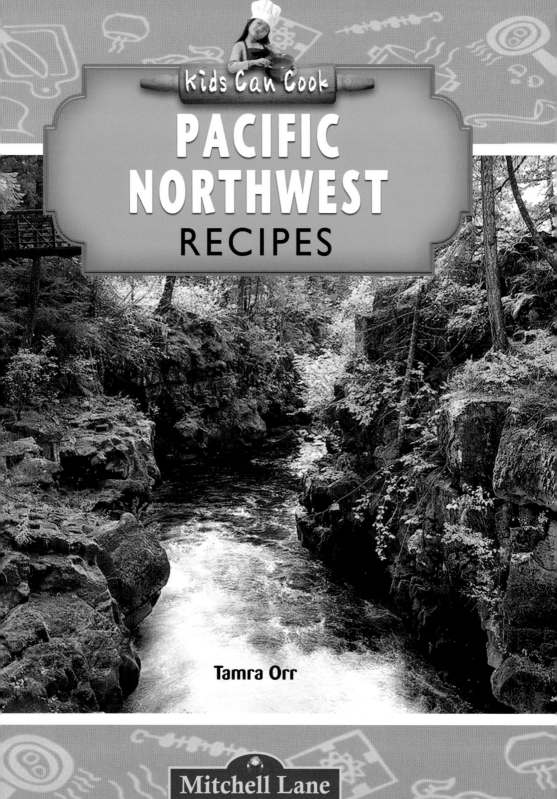

Kids Can Cook

PACIFIC
NORTHWEST
RECIPES

Tamra Orr

Mitchell Lane
PUBLISHERS

Thompson-Nicola Regional District
Library System
300 - 465 VICTORIA STREET
KAMLOOPS, B.C.   V2C 2A9

kids Can Cook

Mid-Atlantic • Midwestern New England • **Pacific Northwest** Southwestern • Western Recipes

Copyright © 2012 by Mitchell Lane Publishers

All rights reserved. No part of this book may be reproduced without written permission from the publisher. Printed and bound in the United States of America.

PUBLISHER'S NOTE: The facts on which the story in this book is based have been thoroughly researched. Documentation of such research can be found on page 60. While every possible effort has been made to ensure accuracy, the publisher will not assume liability for damages caused by inaccuracies in the data, and makes no warranty on the accuracy of the information contained herein.

Library of Congress Cataloging-in-Publication Data
Orr, Tamra.
 Pacific Northwest recipes / by Tamra Orr.
    p. cm.
 Includes bibliographical references and index.
 ISBN 978-1-61228-072-1 (library bound)
 1. Cooking, American—Pacific Northwest
 style. I. Title.
 TX715.2.P32O77 2012
 641.59795--dc23
                                         2011034469

eBook ISBN: 9781612281667

Printing   1   2   3   4   5   6   7   8   9

                                                    PLB

3 5444 00051651 7

THE MENU

When visitors come to the Pacific Northwest states of Oregon and Washington, they often cannot believe how incredibly beautiful the region is. In one direction is the sparkling blue Pacific Ocean, lined with sandy beaches and rocky cliffs. In another direction is the high desert, complete with sagebrush and tumbleweeds.

Heading into the Columbia River Gorge area, which spans the border between these two states, people are awestruck by thick rows of dark green pine trees as far as the eye can see and winding rivers that once led famous explorers to these lands for the first time. Rolling hills full of grape vineyards and fruit and nut orchards compete in the countryside with dense forests and rich fields of crops.

On the region's horizon are mountain ranges topped with bright blankets of white snow almost all year round, from the sharp point of Mount Hood in Oregon to the blunted top of Mount St. Helens in Washington. The bustling cities of Portland and Seattle are also home to hundreds of thousands of people who appreciate the region's wet winters and dry summers. They also relish coffee—and lots of it. There are coffee shops on almost every corner. This is where chains like Starbucks and Seattle's Best got their start.

All of this amazing scenery is more than just beautiful. It is also the reason Pacific Northwest foods and cooking are known all over the

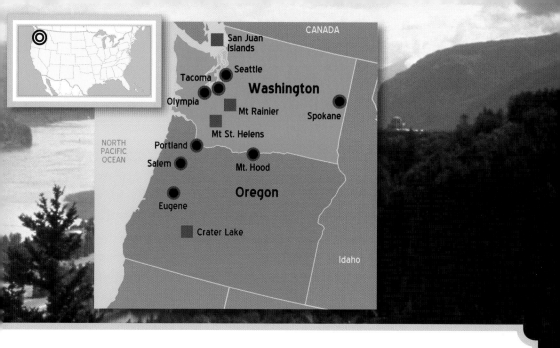

world. The oceans bring a wide variety of exotic seafood to the area, from the popular Chinook salmon to Dungeness crabs and mussels. Rivers and lakes are also teeming with catfish and other foods that make delicious dishes. Forests are home to all kinds of wild mushrooms and truffles. Acres of orchards keep the people supplied with apples and hazelnuts and many other fruits and nuts. Oregon leads the country in the production of several types of berries—from blackberries and raspberries to the unique loganberries and marionberries. Yellow-and-pink Rainier and dark red Bing cherries are local favorites too.

Washington supplies the nation with over half its apple crops. It is also known for its creamy yellow Yukon potatoes and sweet Walla Walla onions. Other crops that grow well in the Pacific Northwest include regular and Jerusalem artichokes and leafy greens such as arugula, sorrel, and spinach.

Just as anyone visiting the Pacific Northwest is sure to find beautiful scenery, so they will also find delicious and unique dishes. Many of them take advantage of the wide variety of foods from the area and, with the right recipes, you can too!

Please work with an adult whenever a recipe calls for using a knife, a stove or oven, or boiling water.

Rose Petal Lemonade

Portland, Oregon, is known as the Rose City. Each year, it hosts the citywide Rose Festival, and one of its biggest conference centers is called the Rose Quarter. Each spring in the city, huge roses burst forth in all shades. Here is a recipe that makes use of those velvety petals. If you don't have roses in your garden or it is the wrong season, you can find dried rose petals in health food stores and gourmet grocers.

Preparation time: 15 minutes
Cooking Time: 30 Minutes
Servings: 8

Ingredients

- 1   cup boiling water
- ¼   cup dried rose petals, or ¾ cup fresh
- 1   cup sugar
- 1   cup fresh-squeezed lemon juice
  Ice to fill a 2-quart pitcher
- 4   cups sparkling water or club soda

1. Have an adult pour the boiling water over the rose petals.
2. Let it steep for ten minutes.
3. Strain the liquid into a pitcher and throw away the rest.
4. Stir in the sugar and lemon juice and continue stirring until the sugar is dissolved.
5. Put a few fresh petals in the pitcher and fill with ice.
6. Finally, pour in the sparkling water.

7

Espresso Ice Cream Soda

Coffee is popular in almost every possible form in the Pacific Northwest, including hot drinks, cold drinks, sauces, and candy. The choices offered in most coffee shops are staggering, with countless combinations. Here is one way to have some coffee as a dessert.

Preparation Time: 30 minutes
Cooking Time: 15 minutes
Serves: 2

Ingredients

- ¾ cup freshly brewed espresso coffee
- ¼ cup sugar
- ½ cup milk
- 1 cup vanilla ice cream
- Soda water as needed

1. Add the sugar to the freshly brewed coffee. Stir to dissolve.
2. Chill until cooled to at least room temperature.
3. Stir in the milk.
4. Fill two tall glasses halfway with the coffee mixture.
5. Add a scoop of ice cream to each glass.
6. Top with soda water.

Parmesan Cheese Crisps

From summer barbecues to winter Super Bowl parties, appetizers are always popular. This one makes the best out of locally made Parmesan cheese.

Preparation time: 5 minutes
Cooking time: 10 minutes
Makes: 16 bite-sized pieces

Ingredients

1   tablespoon olive oil
1   tablespoon flour
1   cup shredded Parmesan cheese

1. Preheat the oven to 350°F.
2. Line a baking sheet with a nonstick pan liner or with baker's parchment. Rub the liner with olive oil.
3. Sprinkle flour over the oil and shake to distribute the flour evenly.
4. Put a tablespoon of the shredded cheese on the baking sheet. Flatten it slightly. Repeat with remaining cheese, allowing $1/2$ inch between the piles.
5. Bake for 10 minutes, or until the cheese is bubbling and slightly browned.
6. Cool for 5 minutes, and then lift the crisps from the sheets with a spatula.
7. Serve at once or keep in an airtight container for several days.

Sun-dried Tomatoes with Basil

The perfect topping for Parmesan cheese crisps uses sun-dried tomatoes and the basil that grows on many farms throughout Washington and Oregon.

Preparation time: 30 minutes
Makes: About one cup

Ingredients

- 1 cup sun-dried tomatoes cut in strips
- 1 cup boiling water
- 1 teaspoon kosher salt
- 1 small bunch (about 4 stems) fresh basil
- $1/2$ cup olive oil
- $1/2$ teaspoon freshly ground black pepper

1. Put the sun-dried tomatoes in a medium mixing bowl, and have an adult cover them with boiling water and salt.
2. Allow the tomatoes and water to stand for 10 minutes or until softened. Most of the water will be absorbed by the tomatoes.
3. Strip the leaves of basil from the stems. Stack the leaves into a small pile on a cutting board.
4. Roll the pile of leaves into a tight bundle. Have an adult cut them with a sharp knife into thin ribbons.
5. Drain the tomatoes of any remaining water.
6. Put the tomatoes in a food processor until they are pureed.
7. Return the tomatoes to the bowl in which they were soaked, and stir in the olive oil and pepper.
8. Serve the sun-dried tomatoes on top of Parmesan cheese crisps or toast.

Corn and Oyster Chowder

With so much of Oregon and Washington's coastline on the Pacific Ocean, it is little surprise that fishermen keep busy all day bringing in their catch, including crab, sea urchins, abalone, and of course, oysters. These delicacies are often used in soups and salads.

Driving down the back roads of the coastal towns, tourists often spot signs advertising fresh oysters—and they mean FRESH. For only a dollar or two, a fisherman will reach into the ocean, haul up a net of oysters, and a few minutes later hand you a cooked oyster ready to eat. Just watch out—they are slippery and often quite hot, and they may come with the warning to "Wait a moment—hold on until the stomach stops boiling." Here is a recipe using those tasty oysters.

Preparation time: 15 minutes
Cooking time: 60 to 70 minutes
Serves: 4

Ingredients

1	tablespoon olive oil
1	medium onion, diced
5	thick slices bacon
2	medium new potatoes, diced
12	medium oysters, scrubbed
3	tablespoons all-purpose flour
1	cup half-and-half
	Salt and freshly ground black pepper
	Kernels from two ears of fresh corn (about 1½ cups)

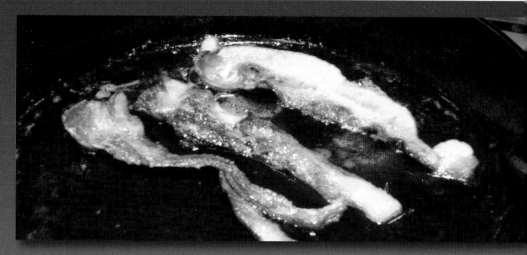

1. Have an adult heat the oil in a large saucepan over medium heat and sauté the onion. Cook it until it is translucent and slightly golden. Set it aside.
2. In a separate skillet, sauté the bacon until crisp. Drain it on paper towels and, when cooled, tear into half-inch pieces.
3. Place the diced potatoes in a saucepan, cover with water, and cook until they can just be pierced with a fork.
4. Drain the potatoes, reserving one cup of the potato water.

5. Place the oysters in a large saucepan with one-fourth cup water. Steam them over high heat until they just open (about 10 minutes). Strain the liquid and reserve.

6. Add the flour to the sautéed onions and, stirring constantly, cook them over medium heat until foamy.

7. Stir in the reserved oyster liquid and potato water and mix well.

8. Add the oysters and the half-and-half.

9. Stir in the corn and the bacon and cook until heated through (do not allow this to come to a boil).

10. Season to taste with salt and pepper. Garnish each serving with chopped parsley.

Pear Chicken Walnut Salad

The restaurants in the Pacific Northwest often make sure to include many different salads on their menus because there is a strong trend toward healthy eating throughout the region. Here is an example of a favorite and vitamin-packed salad.

Preparation time: 30 minutes
Cooking time: 30 minutes
Serves: 4

Ingredients

Salad
$^3/_4$	pound boneless, skinless chicken breasts
$1^1/_2$	cups chicken broth
1	Asian pear, peeled and sliced
1	cup fresh spinach leaves, stems removed
1	head butter lettuce, torn
$^1/_2$	cup chopped walnuts
	Walnut halves for garnish

Dressing
$1^1/_2$	teaspoons Dijon mustard
$^1/_8$	garlic, minced
$^1/_8$	shallot, minced
$^1/_2$	teaspoon fine chopped basil, thyme, or tarragon
1	tablespoon tarragon vinegar
$^1/_4$	cup mild flavored vegetable oil
1	tablespoon fresh lemon juice
$^1/_2$	teaspoon salt and pepper

1. Under adult supervision, bake chicken in broth in a foil-covered pan at 350°F for 30 minutes.

2. Cool and have an adult cut it into strips.
3. Combine dressing ingredients and whisk them together.
4. Combine in a large bowl: pears (reserve a few slices for garnish), spinach, lettuce, and chopped walnuts.
5. Add chicken.
6. Toss with dressing.
7. Divide mixture onto two plates. Garnish with walnut halves and a few pear slices.

Romaine and Apple Salad
with Toasted Walnuts

Many of the people who live in the biggest cities of Oregon and Washington are vegetarians. Quite a few of the restaurants cater to this lifestyle choice. They frequently offer a huge selection of non-meat sandwiches and pasta, plus a full salad menu. Here is an example of a popular salad using local ingredients.

Preparation time: 15 minutes
Cooking time: 20 minutes
Serves: 6

Ingredients

½   cup apple cider
½   cup apple cider vinegar
2   tablespoons sugar
2   teaspoons salt
1   teaspoon freshly ground
     black pepper
¾   cup walnut oil
3   large ripe Jonagold or other crisp, sweet
     apples (1½ pounds)
2   hearts of romaine lettuce, washed, spun dry, and cut into 2-inch
     pieces
6   tablespoons Oregon blue cheese, crumbled
½   cup toasted walnuts

1. In a small saucepan, have an adult boil the apple cider over high heat until it is about half of its original amount. It will be thick like syrup.
2. Take the pan off the heat, add the apple cider vinegar, and stir.
3. Whisk in the sugar, salt, and pepper. Slowly whisk in the walnut oil.

Core the apples and then cut them lengthwise into matchsticks, about a quarter inch thick.

In a large mixing bowl, combine the apples with ¾ cup apple cider dressing, and toss to coat.

Add the lettuce and toss again. Most of the apples will settle to the bottom of the bowl.

Distribute the dressed lettuce and apple matchsticks evenly between six chilled salad plates.

Over each salad, crumble a tablespoon of blue cheese and then scatter a generous tablespoon of toasted walnuts.

Gazpacho

Pacific Northwest summers are often hot and dry, so a summer dish made with garden vegetables is refreshing. Try this cold soup on a hot afternoon and see what you think! It takes a lot of chopping but no time to cook.

Preparation time: 45 minutes + 4 hours to chill
Serves: 12

Ingredients

- 2 pounds vine-ripened tomatoes, diced fine
- 2 cucumbers, peeled and diced fine
- 2 cups V-8 or tomato juice
- ½ Walla Walla or sweet onion, diced
- 1 green bell pepper, cored, seeded and diced fine
- 1 cup loosely packed cilantro leaves
- 2 tablespoons olive oil
- 2 tablespoons vinegar
- 2 large cloves garlic, minced
- 1 tablespoon freshly squeezed lemon juice
- Salt and freshly ground black pepper

1. Combine the tomatoes, cucumbers, V-8 juice, onion, green pepper, cilantro, olive oil, vinegar, garlic, and lemon juice in a large, plastic (not metal) bowl.
2. Season to taste with salt and pepper.
3. Cover and chill at least 4 hours before serving.

Summer Berry Salad

Summertime in the Pacific Northwest also brings berry vines that are so heavy they drop to the ground. Throughout the area, blackberry vines grow almost as you watch them. It is not uncommon to drive down a side road and spot a family picking free berries and munching them as fast as they pick. This salad is a perfect way to put seasonal strawberries to use.

Preparation time: 20 to 30 minutes
Serves: 6 to 8

Ingredients

2	bunches fresh spinach, washed, dried and torn
2	pints fresh strawberries, cleaned and halved
1/3	cup sugar
2	tablespoons sesame seeds
1	tablespoon poppyseeds (optional)
1/4	teaspoon Worcestershire sauce
1/4	teaspoon paprika
1/2	cup vegetable oil
1/4	cup cider vinegar

1. Place spinach and strawberries in a bowl.
2. Place the rest of the ingredients in a blender and blend until mixed and thick.
3. Just before serving, gently toss the salad and dressing together.

Mount Bachelor
Steak Soup

One of Oregon's most scenic mountains is Mount Bachelor, located in the middle of the state. One of several dormant volcanoes in the area, it earned its name because it sits apart from three other mountains named the Three Sisters. Mount Bachelor is a popular ski resort. This warm dish can be served after a long day on the slopes.

Preparation time: 30 minutes
Cooking time: 2 hours
Serves: 6 to 8

Ingredients

1	pound flank or round steak, cut up and browned
½	pound butter or margarine
2	cups flour
8	cups water
1	carrot, chopped
1	onion, chopped
1	celery stalk, chopped
1	12-ounce package frozen mixed vegetables
1	14.5-ounce can tomatoes, chopped
4	tablespoons instant beef bouillon
	Pepper to taste

A roux (pronounced ROO) is a lot like gravy that is used to thicken some dishes, as well as add flavor. It is usually made out of water, butter, and flour. After the butter is melted in the water, the flour is added very slowly, with constant stirring. It takes between 15 and 30 minutes for the roux to darken and thicken. Once it does, remove it from the heat and add it to your stockpot.

1. Have an adult cut the steak into pieces, brown it, and then set it aside.
2. Combine the butter, flour, and 2 cups of water to make a roux.
3. Place the roux in a stockpot and add all the remaining ingredients.
4. Simmer for 1½ to 2 hours and serve!

Salmon Loaf
with Lemon and Parsley Sauce

Mention the word *salmon* anywhere throughout Oregon and Washington and you are likely to get people talking. If they aren't discussing how some types of salmon are being overfished and threatened, they are talking about different recipes to highlight this beloved fish. You will easily spot a dozen or more stores, restaurants, and even medical offices with the word *Chinook* in them in honor of this fish and its long history in the region. Early Native Americans and the Europeans who followed saw the salmon in the rivers and thought that they simply could never run out. Today, people know otherwise.

Salmon is found in appetizers, salads, and main courses and is often a favorite at summer barbecues. Here are two recipes that make the most of this delicately flavored pink fish.

Preparation time: 30 minutes
Cooking time: 40 minutes
Serves: 6

Ingredients

1	cup breadcrumbs
¾	cup milk
½	teaspoon salt
2	tablespoons finely chopped onion
2	tablespoons unsalted butter, melted
2	eggs, slightly beaten
2	cups flaked cooked salmon
3	tablespoons fresh lemon juice
½	teaspoon pepper
2	tablespoons finely chopped celery
1/8	teaspoon grated nutmeg

Sauce

½   cup (1 stick) unsalted butter
⅛   teaspoon salt
2   tablespoons minced fresh parsley
¼   cup fresh lemon juice

1. Preheat the oven to 350°F.
2. In a large mixing bowl, combine the ingredients for the salmon loaf in the order given, mixing well.
3. Oil a loaf pan and press the mixture into the pan. Bake about 40 minutes, or until a knife inserted in the center comes out clean.
4. While the salmon loaf is baking, prepare the sauce. First, melt the butter over medium heat in a saucepan.
5. Whisk in the remaining ingredients.
6. Serve the sauce hot over slices of salmon loaf.

Smoked Salmon Scalloped Potatoes

If you want to sample salmon a different way, see what happens when you use it to dress up traditional scalloped potatoes.

Preparation time: 20 to 25 minutes
Cooking time: 40 minutes
Serves: 6 to 8

Ingredients

10	medium red potatoes, boiled, peeled, and cut into quarter-inch slices
6	ounces smoked salmon, crumbled
6	green onions, diced
3	garlic cloves, minced
	Salt to taste
¾	cup heavy cream
½	cup freshly grated Parmesan cheese

1. Preheat the oven to 350°F.
2. Grease a 9 x 13-inch baking or casserole dish.
3. Place a layer of sliced potatoes in the dish. Sprinkle with one-fourth of the salmon, one-fourth of the onions, and one-fourth of the garlic.
4. Sprinkle with salt and continue layering like this until all of the potatoes, salmon, onions, and garlic are used.
5. Pour the cream over the casserole.
6. Top with grated cheese.
7. Bake for 40 minutes or until golden.

Teriyaki Tuna

Although salmon is the most popular fish in the Pacific Northwest, a number of other types of fish come in a close second. One of those is tuna. It is used in many different kinds of sushi made in area restaurants. Japanese recipes have been a part of the Pacific Northwest's cuisine since the 1880s when thousands of Japanese people came to the region to work on the railroads.

Preparation time: 2½ hours including marination
Cooking time: 5 minutes
Serves: 6

Ingredients

- 1½ to 2 pounds fresh tuna
- 1 cup low-sodium soy sauce
- 2 tablespoons sugar
- 2 cloves garlic, crushed
- ⅔ cup dry sherry
- 1 tablespoon finely chopped ginger root or 1 teaspoon ginger powder

1. Mix first 5 ingredients in a 9 x 13-inch pan.
2. Add tuna and marinate for 2 hours, turning every ½ hour in refrigerator.
3. Under adult supervision, grill on a barbecue for 5 minutes on each side.

Thompson Nicola Regional District Library System

Sweet Pepper Chicken

Of course, just because you are in the Pacific Northwest, it doesn't mean you have to eat seafood. There are many other wonderful choices. If you happen to enjoy chicken, try one of these area favorites.

Preparation time: 15 minutes
Cooking time: 25 to 30 minutes
Serves: 6

Ingredients

3   pounds boneless skinless chicken breasts, cut in half
3   tablespoons butter
3   tablespoons olive oil
    Salt and pepper to taste
3   cloves garlic, minced
1/3 cup finely chopped onion
2   tablespoons chopped fresh parsley
2   red bell peppers, seeded and diced
2   green bell peppers, seeded and diced

1. In a skillet, with the help of an adult, melt two tablespoons butter and two tablespoons olive oil over medium-high heat. Sauté the chicken breasts for four to five minutes on each side until browned.
2. Sprinkle the chicken with salt and pepper, and then remove it from the pan. Set it aside.
3. In the same pan, melt the remaining butter and oil. Add garlic and onion, and sauté over medium heat until the onion is tender and translucent.
4. Add parsley, peppers, and chicken.
5. Cover and simmer for five minutes until the chicken is tender and cooked through.

Chicken and Noodle Casserole

This popular chicken dish is particularly good on a cold, rainy day.

Preparation time: 10 to 15 minutes
Cooking time: 90 to 100 minutes
Serves: 4

Ingredients

2	garlic cloves, minced
2	carrots, diced
1	medium onion, diced
3–4	boneless, skinless chicken breasts, cut into strips
2	teaspoons salt
½	teaspoon freshly grated black pepper
8	cups water
6	ounces fettuccine noodles
½	cup grated sharp cheddar cheese

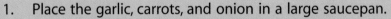

1. Place the garlic, carrots, and onion in a large saucepan.
2. Lay the chicken strips over the vegetables and sprinkle with salt and pepper.
3. Cover with water. Bring the water to a boil and then turn off the heat. Cover the pan for 30 minutes or until cooked through.
4. Remove the chicken from the broth. Reserve 1¼ cups of the broth and the cooked vegetables.
5. Bring 4 cups of water to boil over high heat.
6. Stir in the noodles and cook until just tender, about 3 minutes.
7. Pour the noodles into a colander and rinse under cold running water.

8. Preheat the oven to 375°F. Grease the bottom of a one-quart casserole dish.
9. Scatter one-third of the noodles in the dish. Top with one-third of the chicken.
10. Repeat until the chicken and noodles are used up.
11. Pour the rest of the broth and the vegetables over everything.
12. Cover the casserole and bake for 30 minutes.
13. Uncover and top with cheddar cheese. Have an adult place it under the broiler until the cheese is brown and bubbling.

Northwest Pesto and Noodles

This vegetarian recipe makes the most of the hazelnuts that grow in this part of the country. The spelt noodles add extra protein and can be found at many gourmet grocery or health food stores. Traditional pasta or egg noodles can be used as well.

Preparation time: 10 minutes
Cooking time: 20 to 25 minutes
Serves: 4

Ingredients

2   cups fresh basil
½   cup hazelnut oil
2   small cloves garlic
½   teaspoon salt
½   cup roasted hazelnuts
1/3 cup goat cheese
     (or cheese of your
     choice)
10   ounces spelt noodles
2   tomatoes, chopped

1. Put the fresh basil leaves in a blender with some hazelnut oil. Mix until it starts to turn into a paste.
2. Add garlic and salt and continue to blend.
3. Add hazelnuts and cheese. If more oil is needed, add it also. This is the pesto.
4. Cook the noodles according to the package directions.
5. Drain the noodles.
6. In a skillet, add noodles, five tablespoons of pesto, and tomatoes.
7. Toss and let cook over medium heat for 1 to 2 minutes.

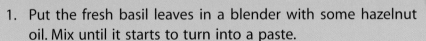

Winter Pot Roast

Winters in the Pacific Northwest are cold and wet. For those who live high in the mountains, blizzards are common, but this snowfall makes snowboarders, skiers, and snowmobilers very happy. At lower levels, in cities such as Seattle and Portland, the winter weather usually takes the form of endless days of rain. On days like this, a cup of hot stew or bowl of pot roast hits the spot. Although wine is used in the recipe, all of the alcohol cooks off during the hours in the oven. If alcohol is not permitted in your home, you can use beef stock in place of the wine.

Preparation time: 20 minutes
Cooking time: 3 hours
Serves: 6 to 8

Ingredients

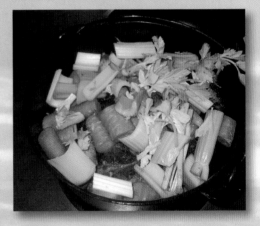

3–4	pounds beef pot roast
	Olive oil
4–8	carrots, chopped
3–6	celery stalks, chopped
3	onions, chopped
1	bay leaf
2	cloves garlic, chopped
	Salt and pepper to taste
2	cups dry red wine or beef stock
	Water

1. Preheat the oven to 325°F.
2. Have an adult place the olive oil in a skillet on medium heat. Brown the sides of the roast thoroughly, approximately 5 to 10 minutes.
3. Place the roast in a Dutch oven and add chopped carrots, celery, and onions.
4. Add the spices and red wine or beef stock.
5. Cover tightly and bake for three hours. The roast is done when the meat pulls apart easily.
6. Approximately an hour and a half into baking, check the liquid level. If it looks like less than half full, add water.

Baked Butternut Squash
with Hazelnuts

A bounty of fertile soil, spring rains, and summer sunshine all combine to help the Pacific Northwest grow some of the best fruit orchards and vegetable crops in the country. Many fabulous side dishes make the most of local specialties such as Yukon Gold potatoes, butternut squash, artichokes, kale, and yams.

Virtually all of the hazelnuts in the United States are grown in Oregon. In fact, 98 percent of the nation's supply comes from the more than 3.75 million trees in the western part of this state. Hazelnuts are also known as filberts. Here is a wonderful recipe that blends these crunchy nuts with a creamy squash—a terrific combination.

Preparation time: 5 minutes
Cooking time: 40 minutes
Serves: 6

Ingredients

2	butternut squash, cut in half lengthwise
5	tablespoons unsalted butter
½	teaspoon salt
¼	freshly ground black pepper
½	cup chopped toasted hazelnuts (see directions for toasting them in the Orange-Hazelnut Biscotti recipe on page 48)

1. Preheat the oven to 375°F.
2. Bake the squash, cut side down, on a baking sheet for about 40 minutes or until tender.
3. Allow the squash to cool slightly. When it is easy to handle, use a spoon to scoop out the seeds.
4. Scrape the squash flesh into a mixing bowl. Mash with a potato masher.
5. Add the butter, salt, and pepper, mixing well.

6. Spoon the squash into a serving dish. Garnish with the toasted hazelnuts.

Artichoke Rice

Another big favorite in the Pacific Northwest is artichokes. If you are used to seeing artichoke hearts packed with oil in a jar, you may not know that they start out as huge leafy vegetables. One of the best ways to enjoy these unusual-looking vegetables is by steaming them and then peeling off each leaf, dipping it in butter, and scraping the inner side of the leaf with your teeth. It is a slow but enjoyable process. Once all the leaves are pulled off, you get to the base of the vegetable. Inside the base is the heart, which is soft and buttery. Add marinated artichoke hearts to this simple dish to make it fancy.

Preparation time: 5 minutes
Cooking time: 45 to 60 minutes (varies by the rice chosen)
Serves: 4 to 6

Ingredients

- 1 (6-ounce) package chicken-flavored rice
- 2 (6½-ounce) jars marinated artichoke hearts (with liquid)
- ⅓ cup mayonnaise
- ¾ teaspoon curry powder
- 4 green onions, sliced
- ½ green pepper, chopped
- 12 stuffed green olives, sliced

1. Cook rice according to package instructions. Remove pan from heat.
2. Drain and chop artichokes, but keep the juice.
3. In a small container, blend artichoke juice, mayonnaise, and curry powder.
4. Stir marinade mixture into rice. Add chopped artichokes, onions, green pepper, and olives; toss well. May be served warm or cold.

Whipped Yukon Gold Potatoes

Another one of the Pacific Northwest's treats are the creamy, rich Yukon Gold potatoes. They are used in casseroles and soups and as a delicious side dish like this one.

Preparation time: 15 minutes
Cooking time: 20 minutes
Makes: About 12 cups

Ingredients

5	pounds Yukon Gold potatoes
1	tablespoon salt
¼	cup canola oil

1. Scrub the potatoes thoroughly and have an adult dice them into one-inch pieces.
2. Put the diced potatoes and salt in a heavy, one-gallon stockpot.
3. Add water to barely cover. Bring to a boil over high heat. Reduce the heat to low and cook the potatoes until they are quite tender and beginning to fall apart (approximately 15 minutes).
4. Place a colander in a bowl and have the adult drain the potatoes. Save the cooking liquid.
5. Put the potatoes back in the stockpot and whisk in the canola oil, mashing the potatoes in the process.
6. Whisk in just enough of the reserved cooking liquid to make the mashed potatoes smooth and creamy. Put in a serving bowl and top with butter.

Sautéed Kale with Garlic

Kale is a popular green in the Pacific Northwest, where people grow it on porches and in backyard gardens. Even ornamental kale, which is a deep green and purple, can be found in people's yards and landscaping. Kale is very nutritious, packing high amounts of vitamins such as A, C, K, and B_6, plus fiber, calcium, and potassium. Here is an easy way to fix this hearty vegetable.

Preparation time: 10 minutes
Cooking time: 5 minutes
Serves: 2 to 3

Ingredients

1	bunch of curly green kale
2	tablespoons olive oil
4	cloves garlic, sliced
½	teaspoon salt
¼	teaspoon freshly ground black pepper

1. Rinse the kale and shake off the excess water.
2. Stack the leaves with all the stems pointed in the same direction. Then roll them lengthwise into a tight bundle.
3. Have an adult trim the stems and cut the bundle crosswise into quarter-inch ribbons.
4. Put the olive oil in a saucepan over high heat.
5. Add the garlic, salt, and pepper, and then add the kale.
6. Cook for one to two minutes, moving the greens quickly around in the pan until they are wilted.
7. Remove from heat and serve at once.

Summer Vegetable Pot

Lovely Pacific Northwest summers full of sunshine result in an abundance of healthy gardens. Some of the most commonly grown vegetables can be combined in this dish and enjoyed together.

Preparation time: 15 minutes
Cooking time: 45 minutes
Serves: 6 to 8

Ingredients

- 4 ears fresh corn
- 5 medium tomatoes, cut in quarter-inch slices
- 6 small zucchini, each cut lengthwise into four pieces
- 2 medium onions, sliced in thin rings
- 2 cloves garlic, minced
  Salt and pepper to taste
  Lemon pepper to taste
- ½ cup butter

1. Preheat the oven to 325°F.
2. Cut the corn from the cob.
3. Put the corn, tomatoes, zucchini, and onions into a large casserole dish.
4. Add garlic, salt, pepper, and lemon pepper.
5. Mix everything together and then dot with butter.
6. Bake for 45 minutes. Serve hot.

Orange Hazelnut Biscotti

Have you ever tried biscotti? There is a secret to eating this crunchy, hard cookie. It needs to be dipped into a hot beverage first. For many people in the Pacific Northwest, that means sharing a piece of biscotti with a cup of hot coffee, but you can also use hot apple cider or hot chocolate. Stop by a regional coffee shop and you are sure to see a display case of different flavors of biscotti sitting by the cash register. Give this recipe a try and see what you think!

Preparation time: 15 minutes
Cooking time: 50 minutes
Makes: About 30 pieces

Ingredients

4	cups unbleached white flour
1	tablespoon baking powder
½	teaspoon salt
1	cup unsalted butter
1½	cups sugar
1½	tablespoons orange zest, finely chopped
2	eggs
1	tablespoon vanilla extract
1	tablespoon orange flavoring
1	cup toasted hazelnuts

1. Preheat the oven to 350°F.
2. Distribute nuts evenly over a cookie sheet in a single layer. Toast in the oven and have an adult stir them occasionally, until they are brown (approximately 10 to 15 minutes). Let them cool.
3. In a small bowl, stir together the flour, baking powder, and salt and set aside.

4. In a large mixing bowl, cream together the butter, sugar, and orange zest.
5. Add the eggs, vanilla, and orange flavoring and beat until well blended.
6. Stir in the dry ingredients until just blended, and then stir in the nuts.
7. Roll the dough into a log. It should be one inch high and two to three inches wide.
8. Bake for 25 minutes, until lightly browned.
9. Let the log cool for about 10 minutes. Adjust the oven temperature to 300°F.
10. Have an adult slice the log diagonally into half-inch cookies.
11. Return cookies to the baking sheet and cook them in the oven for 10 minutes on each side. Let them cool, and they are ready to eat!

Yogurt Huckleberry Muffins

The Pacific Northwest is known for growing many different kinds of berries, including the sweet, tangy huckleberry. Huckleberry muffins make the perfect afternoon treat. If you cannot find huckleberries in your store, substitute blueberries for them.

Preparation time: 15 minutes
Cooking time: 15 minutes
Makes: 12 muffins

Ingredients

6	tablespoons unsalted butter, softened
1	cup plus 2 tablespoons sugar
3	large eggs
2	cups sifted unbleached all-purpose flour
½	teaspoon baking soda
¼	teaspoon salt
1	cup plus 2 tablespoons plain yogurt
½	teaspoon vanilla extract
1½	cups huckleberries

1. Preheat the oven to 425°F, and grease a 12-cup muffin tin (or use muffin papers).
2. In a mixing bowl, cream together the butter and sugar until pale and fluffy.
3. Add the eggs one at a time, mixing well.
4. Sift together the flour, baking soda, and salt.
5. Add the flour mixture to the egg mixture, alternating with the yogurt.
6. Stir in the vanilla and berries.
7. Fill each muffin cup two-thirds full with batter.
8. Bake for about 15 minutes, or until lightly browned on top.

Oregon Blueberry Walnut Cobbler

Many families in Oregon and Washington consider blueberry season, which is in midsummer, one of the best times of the year. Heading out into the country, they find the closest blueberry patch, grab a large white bucket or wicker basket, and head down the rows to pick scads of blueberries. They take them home, wash them, and then either freeze them, eat them right away, or make a delicious dessert like this one.

Preparation time: 15 to 20 minutes
Cooking time: 15 minutes
Serves: 8 to 10

Ingredients

- ½ cup sugar
- 1 tablespoon cornstarch
- 4 cups Oregon blueberries
- 2 tablespoons water
- 1 cup Bisquick baking mix
- ¼ cup milk
- ¼ cup Oregon walnuts
- 1 tablespoon sugar
- 1 tablespoon butter, melted

1. Preheat the oven to 425°F.
2. Mix sugar and cornstarch in a saucepan.
3. Stir in the berries and water. Boil and stir for one minute.
4. Pour into a baking dish.
5. In another bowl, stir the remaining ingredients to make a soft dough. Drop by tablespoonful onto hot filling.
6. Bake for 15 minutes.

Marionberry Pie

If you've never heard of marionberries, don't be surprised. If you don't live in the Pacific Northwest, you may have never seen or tasted one. In Oregon and Washington, this fruit is added to ice creams, jellies and jams, and pies. They are a hybrid—a cross between blackberries and raspberries—developed in Oregon in 1965. Today, half of the blackberries produced in the state are marionberries. They are transported throughout the country, and you can usually find them in the grocery store's frozen food section. Some stores also sell marionberry jelly. If you can't find any marionberries, you can make this recipe with blackberries instead.

Preparation time: 30 minutes
Cooking time: 50 minutes
Serves: 8

Ingredients

For filling:
- ½ cup honey
- ¼ cup tapioca flour
- Dash of salt
- 6 cups marionberries

For crust:
- 1½ cups all-purpose flour
- ½ teaspoon salt
- ⅓ cup extra light olive oil
- 4 tablespoons cold milk

For filling:
1. Place a large baking sheet in the oven on the bottom rack and preheat to 375°F.
2. Combine the honey, tapioca flour, and salt in a measuring cup.
3. Stir the honey mixture into the berries.

For crust:
1. Combine flour and salt in a bowl.
2. Measure the olive oil in a one-cup measuring cup.
3. Put the milk in the cup with the oil.
4. Add the oil and milk to the dry ingredients. Stir with a fork until it can be formed into a ball.
5. Form half of the dough into a ball and put it on a 12-inch sheet of wax paper. Flatten it with your hand and put another sheet of wax paper on top.
6. Roll the dough out to the edges of the paper.
7. Remove the top sheet of paper and fit the dough into the pie plate.
8. Fill the pie shell with the marionberry filling.
9. Roll out the second half of the dough like you did the first. Put in on top of the pie and seal the edges with a fork. Cut a few slits in the top to let it bubble.
10. Place the pie on a middle rack in the oven and bake for 50 minutes.

Braised Chestnuts and Brussels Sprouts

Just like every other region in the United States, the Pacific Northwest celebrates the usual holidays each year. They like to celebrate them with special foods like the ones included here. Bring a little Oregon and Washington to your house this year by including one of these recipes.

Along with being the biggest hazelnut growers in the country, Oregon and Washington also produce a great deal of chestnuts. In fact, growing in the town of Sherwood, Oregon, is the largest recorded chestnut tree in the entire United States. Its trunk is 6 feet in diameter— that's almost 19 feet around! Chestnuts can be found online and at gourmet grocery stores across the country. This recipe is a little complicated, but the finished product is well worth it.

Preparation time: 20 minutes
Cooking time: 20 to 25 minutes
Serves: 6

Ingredients

1   pound fresh chestnuts (about 36)
1   pound Brussels sprouts
2   quarts water
2   tablespoons salt
1   cup chicken or vegetable broth

1. Put on a large pot of water to boil the chestnuts.
2. Have an adult use a sharp paring knife to cut an X in the shell of each chestnut. Try not to cut down into the meat of the nut, but do cut through the shell so that the nuts will be easy to peel when they are roasted.
3. Boil the cut chestnuts for 5 minutes. Have an adult scoop them out of the water with a strainer or slotted spoon.

4. While the chestnuts are still hot, carefully pull off the outer shells. Peel off as much of the inner skin as you can. If some of the nuts will not give up their skins, you can reheat them and try again, or have an adult cut away any stubborn pieces with a paring knife.
5. Once again, have an adult trim the bottoms from the Brussels sprouts. Pull away any loose or damaged leaves.
6. Put two quarts of water and the salt in a large saucepan, and bring to a boil.
7. Add the Brussels sprouts and boil for 4 to 5 minutes, or until they can be easily pierced with a fork.
8. Drain the sprouts and rinse in cold water to halt the cooking process.
9. Put the peeled chestnuts in a large sauté pan with the broth and simmer gently for 5 minutes. Do not let the broth boil too hard. This can cause the chestnuts to fall apart.
10. When the chestnuts are tender, add the Brussels sprouts and cook uncovered for another 5 minutes. If the sauce has not turned into a syrupy glaze around the chestnuts and Brussels sprouts, lift the vegetables out with a slotted spoon. Boil the broth in the pan until it is almost gone, then return the vegetables to the pan and toss them to coat them evenly.

Orange Yams Colonial

This tasty side dish is popular at holidays such as Easter, Thanksgiving, and Christmas, but it is delicious year round. If you aren't familiar with yams, they are the same thing as sweet potatoes. Often they are combined with marshmallows, but that can make them too sweet for some people. To keep the taste of the yams and add a gentle sweetness, try combining them with honey and oranges, as in this recipe.

Preparation time: 10 minutes
Cooking time: 1 hour
Serves: 10 to 12

Ingredients

- 4 pounds yams
- 1 tablespoon butter
- 1 tablespoon honey
  Salt, pepper, and nutmeg to taste
  Juice of two oranges, but the rind of only one, grated

1. Wash the yams.
2. Have an adult boil the yams in a covered pan of water until they are tender.
3. Drain them and then drop them in cold water.
4. Slip off the skins, then mash them and blend them with the butter, honey, salt, pepper, nutmeg, orange juice, and rind.
5. Spoon into buttered casserole dish.
6. Bake at 325°F for about 40 minutes until golden.

If you can't actually take a trip to the beautiful states of Oregon and Washington, you might be able to imagine being there after making a few of the region's traditional dishes. As you take a bite, close your eyes and imagine. Perhaps you can smell the fresh scent of the pine trees, feel the icy mountain snow, or hear the cry of the seagulls already . . .

Further Reading

Books

Brown, Cynthia. *Geology of the Pacific Northwest: Investigate How the Earth Was Formed with 15 Projects.* Chicago: Nomad Press, 2011.

Hopkinson, Deborah. *Apples to Oregon: Being the (Slightly) True Narrative of How a Brave Pioneer Father Brought Apples, Peaches, Pears, Plums, Grapes, and Cherries (and Children) Across the Plains.* New York: Aladdin Books, 2008.

Vegetarians of Washington. *Vegetarian Pacific Northwest.* Bellevue, Washington: Healthy Living Publications, 2008.

Works Consulted

Atkinson, Greg. *Entertaining in the Northwest Style.* Seattle, Washington: Sasquatch Books, 2005.

Junior League of Eugene, Oregon. *Savor the Flavor of Oregon.* Eugene: Junior League of Eugene Publishers, 1990.

Lombard, Janelle. *Main Course Salads for Two from the Pacific Northwest.* Bend, Oregon: Lombard Publishing, 2003.

Nims, Cynthia, and Lori McKean. *The Northwest Best Places Cookbook.* Seattle, Washington: Sasquatch Books, 1996.

Skott, Michael, and Lori McKean. *Pacific Northwest Flavors.* New York: Clarkson N. Potter, 1995.

On the Internet

About the Pacific Northwest Region
http://www.nbii.gov/portal/server.pt/community/pacific_northwest/241
Pacific Northwest Region Recipes
http://whatscookingamerica.net/AmericanRegionalFoods/
PacificNorthwest.htm
"A Taste of Seattle"
http://www.sfgate.com/cgi-bin/article.cgi?file=/chronicle/
archive/2001/10/21/TR126327.DTL

PHOTO CREDITS: Cover, pp. 1, 2, 11, 12, 13, 15, 24, 26, 36, 45, 49, 50, 53, 55, 57—CreativeCommons 2.0; pp. 4, 7, 9, 19, 23, 26, 33, 38, 40, 47, 59, 60—Photos.com. All other photos—Tamra Orr. Every effort has been made to locate all copyright holders of material used in this book. If any errors or omissions have occurred, corrections will be made in future editions of the book.

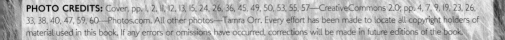

appetizer (AA-peh-ty-zer)—Food or drink served before a meal or as the first course.

baker's parchment (PARCH-munt)—A special type of paper used by bakers to keep food from sticking to the baking pan.

biscotti (bis-KAH-tee)—A crisp Italian cookie that often contains nuts.

bouillon (BULL-yon)—A clear, seasoned broth.

braise (BRAYZ)—To cook slowly in oil and a little bit of some other liquid, such as water or broth.

colander (KAH-lun-der)—A bowl-shaped strainer used for washing and draining foods.

dice—To cut into cubes.

garnish (GAR-nish)—To make a dish look better by adding decorative pieces of raw fruits or vegetables.

marinate (MAYR-ih-nayt)—To soak in a sauce.

mince (MINTZ)—To cut or chop into very small pieces.

puree (pyoor-AY)—To run through a strainer or process in a blender until smooth.

roux (ROO)—A mixture of fat and flour heated and used as a base for sauces and soups.

sauté (saw-TAY)—To fry briefly in a small amount of oil over high heat.

spelt (SPELT)—A type of wheat used to make noodles and bread.

steep (STEEP)—To soak until thoroughly wet or saturated.

whisk (WISK)—To whip food using a stiff, wire-loop tool.

Index

About the
AUTHOR

Tamra Orr is a full-time writer and author living in the Pacific Northwest. She and her family moved to Oregon in 2001, and she became an immediate fan of its cuisine. It wasn't until their arrival on the West Coast that she learned to love coffee. Orr and her husband, as well as their children, enjoyed sampling every recipe in this book and have already made several of them repeatedly. The Winter Pot Roast is a whole family favorite and everyone has taken turns making it. With two hungry teenage sons, Orr has to battle to get a serving of whatever she makes, but when she manages it, she enjoys all of the unique flavors of the Pacific Northwest.